# Non-Perching Birds

## GRAHAM MEADOWS & CLAIRE VIAL

## Contents

Introduction . . . . . . . . . . . . . . . . . . . . . . . . . . . . . . . . . . . . 2
Ratites . . . . . . . . . . . . . . . . . . . . . . . . . . . . . . . . . . . . . . . . 4
Penguins . . . . . . . . . . . . . . . . . . . . . . . . . . . . . . . . . . . . . . 6
Pelicans and Their Relatives . . . . . . . . . . . . . . . . . . . . . . . . 8
Herons and Their Relatives . . . . . . . . . . . . . . . . . . . . . . . . . 9
Waterfowl . . . . . . . . . . . . . . . . . . . . . . . . . . . . . . . . . . . . 10
Flamingos . . . . . . . . . . . . . . . . . . . . . . . . . . . . . . . . . . . . 12
Eagles and Their Relatives . . . . . . . . . . . . . . . . . . . . . . . . 13
Owls . . . . . . . . . . . . . . . . . . . . . . . . . . . . . . . . . . . . . . . . 14
Pheasants, Fowls, and Their Relatives . . . . . . . . . . . . . . . . 15
Gulls and Their Relatives . . . . . . . . . . . . . . . . . . . . . . . . . . 16
Cranes and Their Relatives . . . . . . . . . . . . . . . . . . . . . . . . 18
Pigeons and Doves . . . . . . . . . . . . . . . . . . . . . . . . . . . . . . 19
Parrots . . . . . . . . . . . . . . . . . . . . . . . . . . . . . . . . . . . . . . 20
Kingfishers and Their Relatives . . . . . . . . . . . . . . . . . . . . . 22
Toucans and Their Relatives . . . . . . . . . . . . . . . . . . . . . . . 23
Glossary . . . . . . . . . . . . . . . . . . . . . . . . . . . . . . . . . . . . . 24
Index . . . . . . . . . . . . . . . . . . . . . . . . . . . . . . . . . . . . . . . 24

## DOMINIE PRESS
Pearson Learning Group

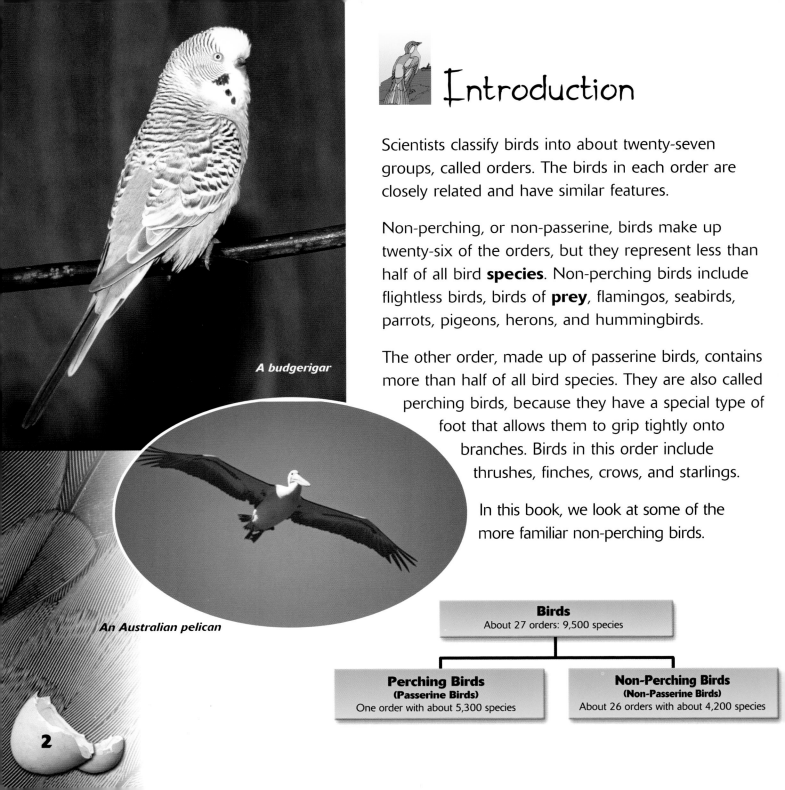

_A budgerigar_

_An Australian pelican_

# Introduction

Scientists classify birds into about twenty-seven groups, called orders. The birds in each order are closely related and have similar features.

Non-perching, or non-passerine, birds make up twenty-six of the orders, but they represent less than half of all bird **species**. Non-perching birds include flightless birds, birds of **prey**, flamingos, seabirds, parrots, pigeons, herons, and hummingbirds.

The other order, made up of passerine birds, contains more than half of all bird species. They are also called perching birds, because they have a special type of foot that allows them to grip tightly onto branches. Birds in this order include thrushes, finches, crows, and starlings.

In this book, we look at some of the more familiar non-perching birds.

**Birds**
About 27 orders: 9,500 species

**Perching Birds**
**(Passerine Birds)**
One order with about 5,300 species

**Non-Perching Birds**
**(Non-Passerine Birds)**
About 26 orders with about 4,200 species

*A triangular-spotted pigeon*

# Ratites

Ratites include five orders of birds: ostriches, rheas, cassowaries, emus, and kiwis. All of these birds are flightless. The ten species of ratites are found only on **continents** in the **Southern Hemisphere**.

The word *ratite* comes from the Latin term for *raft*. Unlike birds that fly, ratites have a flat, raftlike breastbone.

All ratites nest on the ground. All are **omnivorous**. They feed on plants and **invertebrates**.

Ostriches are the largest living birds. They can run up to forty-five miles an hour.

All kiwis are **endangered**. They are mainly **nocturnal**. They lay the largest eggs, in relation to their body size.

*An ostrich*

*A cassowary*

4

*A brown kiwi*

*An emu*

| Order | Distribution | Number of Species | Maximum Height (feet) | Maximum Weight (pounds) | Group Structure | Number of Toes |
|---|---|---|---|---|---|---|
| Ostriches | Africa—grasslands and savannas | 1 | 8 | 150 | Flocks | 2 |
| Rheas | South America—grasslands | 2 | 5 | 45 | Flocks | 3 |
| Cassowaries | Northern Australia and New Guinea—tropical forests | 3 | 5 | 100 | Pairs | 3 |
| Emus | Southern Australia—grasslands | 1 | 6 | 100 | Loose flocks | 3 |
| Kiwis | New Zealand—forests | 3 | 1 ¼ | 8 | Pairs | 4 |

Emperor penguins spend their entire lives in Antarctica.

Yellow-eyed penguin on a nest

 # Penguins

Most scientists believe there are seventeen species of penguins. All penguins are flightless, but they are excellent swimmers. They virtually "fly" through the water. Penguins are found only in the Southern Hemisphere, along the coastlines of Africa, South America, Australia, New Zealand, and **Antarctica**. They feed mainly on fish, squid, and shrimp.

Penguins have a **streamlined**, torpedo-shaped body, with stiff, paddlelike flippers and a short, stubby tail. Their webbed feet and heavy, solid bones help them to swim under water. They have stiff, water-resistant feathers on their bodies. To protect them from the fierce cold, they have down feathers and a thick layer of fat underneath their skin.

*The little blue penguin is the smallest of all penguins.*

*Like most penguins, African penguins form colonies.*

*An Australasian gannet*

# Pelicans and Their Relatives

This order of birds contains about sixty-five species and includes tropical birds, pelicans, gannets, boobies, cormorants, and frigate birds. All birds in this order are **aquatic**. They are found along coastlines worldwide. Pelicans and cormorants are also found inland on rivers and lakes. Their **diet** is made up mainly of fish. They nest in **colonies** on cliffs or in trees.

*A brown pelican*

*A white stork*

# Herons and Their Relatives

There are about 119 species of birds in this order, including herons, storks, bitterns, ibises, and spoonbills. They nest in colonies and live in freshwater **habitats** throughout the world. They all have long legs to help them wade in shallow water. Their diet includes fish, amphibians, reptiles, invertebrates, and plants. Most species feed alone because other birds may disturb their prey.

*A great egret*

*A scarlet ibis*

9

*The European eider is a sea duck.*

# Waterfowl

This order of birds includes screamers, ducks, geese, and swans. Most of the approximately 150 species of birds in this order live in freshwater habitats and **estuaries** throughout the world. Some are found at sea. Waterfowl are powerful fliers. Some species **migrate** thousands of miles. Their diet includes plants and small invertebrates.

*A mute swan*

*The black-necked swan is native to South America.*

The ruddy duck of North America is a diving duck.

The Canada goose is one of many bird species that migrate.

11

# Flamingos

There are five species of flamingos. They nest in colonies in tropical and **subtropical** regions. Flamingos are large, long-legged, and long-necked wading birds. Some feed in shallow water along the edge of the sea. Others feed in saltwater lakes.

A flamingo sifts water through its beak to catch tiny shrimp and plants. A flamingo's pink color is a result of the food it eats.

*The Andean flamingo is native to South America.*

*In Africa, flamingos can form flocks of several million birds.*

12

*This harrier hawk is feeding on a pheasant.*

*Black eagle talons*

# Eagles and Their Relatives

This order of birds includes eagles, hawks, kites, buzzards, vultures, and falcons. They are birds of prey that hunt during the day. There are about 300 species of birds in this order. They are found throughout the world, except in the **Arctic** and in Antarctica.

All the birds in this order have a strong, hooked beak and large feet with sharp claws, called talons. Most of them hunt and kill animals for food, including fish, reptiles, and invertebrates.

*The lappet-faced vulture is the largest vulture in the world.*

13

# Owls

Owls are birds of prey that hunt mainly at night. They are found throughout the world, except in Antarctica. They live mainly in grassland and woodland habitats. Most of the approximately 205 species in this order feed on small **mammals**, birds, or invertebrates.

Owls have large, forward-facing eyes, and they can turn their head around to look behind them. They also have excellent hearing.

*A spotted eagle owl*

*A barn owl*

*The chukar partridge is found in many countries.*

*Male Indian peafowl are called peacocks.*

 # Pheasants, Fowls, and Their Relatives

This order covers about 280 species and includes turkeys, partridges, quail, grouse, and guinea fowl. Members of this order are found throughout the world, except in Antarctica. Males are usually more brightly colored than females.

*The domestic chicken is descended from African jungle fowl. It is one of the most common domestic birds.*

15

The avocet has a curved beak.

# Gulls and Their Relatives

This order contains about 340 species and includes gulls and their relatives. It includes terns, sandpipers, plovers, stilts, and jacanas. Various species are found in most parts of the world, along shorelines and in **wetlands**. Many species feed near the water's edge, probing for invertebrates.

*Jacanas are also called lily-trotters because they can walk on water lily leaves and other floating vegetation.*

Black-backed gulls are often found by the seashore.

White-fronted terns nest in colonies on cliffs.

# Cranes and Their Relatives

This order of birds includes cranes, rails, bustards, trumpeters, and sun bitterns. About 200 species are found throughout the world, except in the Arctic and in Antarctica, in habitats ranging from dense forests to high mountains. They feed on the ground, eating plants and invertebrates.

*The kori bustard is one of the heaviest flying birds in the world.*

*The buff-banded rail is more often heard than seen.*

*The Victoria crowned pigeon is one of the largest pigeons in the world.*

 # Pigeons and Doves

Larger birds in this order are usually known as pigeons, and the smaller ones as doves. They are commonly seen in cities and in the countryside. Pigeons and doves often roost together in groups. Most of the approximately 309 species feed on the fruits and seeds of plants.

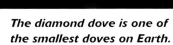

*The diamond dove is one of the smallest doves on Earth.*

19

The golden conure of Brazil is endangered because of loss of habitat and capture for the pet trade.

The black parrot is found only in Madagascar and on the Seychelles Islands.

# Parrots

This order includes parrots, macaws, parakeets, cockatoos, cockatiels, lorikeets, and budgerigars. There are about 354 species of birds in this order. They are found in warmer areas of the world, especially in tropical forests. Most are brightly colored, with a large head, short neck, and hooked beak. They use their hooked beak to crack nuts, hold objects, and climb. Their diet includes seeds, nuts, fruits, nectar, and flowers.

Parrots have two toes pointing forward and two toes pointing backward. This arrangement helps them climb and hold objects.

The hyacinth macaw of South America is the largest macaw in the world.

*The sulphur-crested cockatoo of Australia has a yellow crest.*

*The yellow-bibbed lory is found only on the Solomon Islands.*

21

# Kingfishers and Their Relatives

This order includes kingfishers, bee-eaters, rollers, and hornbills. About 190 species are found worldwide, mainly in woodlands. They nest alone in holes, in either earthen banks or trees. These birds feed on a variety of small animals, including fish, frogs, and invertebrates. Hornbills also eat fruit.

**White-fronted Bee-eater**

*Unlike their name suggests, not all kingfishers eat fish.*

*The toco toucan has one of the largest and brightest beaks in the kingdom of birds.*

# Toucans and Their Relatives

This order includes toucans, honey guides, barbets, and woodpeckers. All are found in trees. About 380 species are found throughout the world in **temperate** and tropical areas. They are not found in **Australasia**, the Arctic, or in Antarctica. They feed mainly on invertebrates and fruit. Like parrots, they have two toes pointing forward and two pointing backward.

*The red-and-yellow barbet often makes its nest in termite mounds.*

23

# Glossary

**Antarctica**: A largely uninhabited continent surrounding the South Pole

**aquatic**: Growing or living in water

**Arctic**: The cold, barren region surrounding the North Pole

**Australasia**: A region southeast of Asia and south of the equator made up of Australia, Tasmania, New Zealand, and Melanesia

**colonies**: Groups of animals of the same kind that live together

**continents**: The largest land masses on Earth; there are seven continents—Africa, Antarctica, Asia, Australia, Europe, North America, and South America

**diet**: The food that an animal or a person usually eats

**endangered**: Threatened with extinction

**estuaries**: Coastal areas where seawater mixes with freshwater from rivers

**habitats**: The places where animals and plants live and grow

**invertebrates**: Animals that do not have a backbone

**mammals**: A class of warm-blooded animals in which the female feeds her young with her own milk

**migrate**: To move from one region or habitat to another in response to cyclical seasonal changes

**nocturnal**: Active at night

**omnivorous**: Surviving on a diet of plants and animals

**prey (n)**: Animals that are hunted and eaten by other animals

**Southern Hemisphere**: The half of Earth located south of the equator

**species**: A group of animals or plants that have many physical characteristics in common

**streamlined**: A shape that offers least resistance when moving through the air or water

**subtropical**: Describing areas of land or sea that are located between tropical and temperate regions

**temperate**: Mild; marked by a moderate climate

**tropical**: Describing areas of land or sea that are very warm throughout the year

**wetlands**: Marshes, swamps, or other areas of land where the soil near the surface is saturated or covered with water, often forming an ideal habitat for a variety of wildlife

# Index

colonies, 7, 8, 9, 12, 17
cranes, 18
doves, 19
eagles, 13
estuaries, 10

flamingos, 2, 12
gulls, 16, 17
herons, 2, 9
invertebrates, 4, 9, 10, 13, 14, 16, 18, 22, 23

kingfishers, 22
owls, 14
parrots, 2, 20, 23
passerine birds, 2
pelicans, 2, 8
penguins, 6, 7
perching birds, 2

pheasant, 13
pigeons, 2, 3, 19
ratites, 4
Southern Hemisphere, 4, 6

talons, 13
toucans, 23
tropical regions, 5, 12, 20
waterfowl, 10
wetlands, 16